My New York City Travel Journal

A Cityscape Kids Journal

Copyright 2018

This Journal Belongs To:

If Founds, Please Return To:

part 1: Trip Notes

Getting There

Travel Dates:

Travel by:

Other _____

Who I'm Traveling With:

Best Part of traveling to New York City:

Things I Need To Pack

Clothes & Accessories:

Entertainment:

Everything Else:

Planned Itinerary

Around the City

Arrival Time:

Travel by:

Other _____

Where I'm Staying:

What I'm Looking Forward to the most:

In The City

First Impressions:

Sights, Sounds, Smells:

Weather:

Check Off Places Visited

- ☐ Central Park
- ☐ Statue of Liberty & Ellis Island
- ☐ The High Line
- ☐ Times Square
- ☐ Broadway and Theater District
- ☐ Washington Square Park
- ☐ New York Public Library
- ☐ The Metropolitan Museum of Art
- ☐ Empire State Building
- ☐ American Museum of Natural History
- ☐ Brooklyn Bridge
- ☐ Museum of Modern Art
- ☐ Yankee Stadium
- ☐ Citi Field
- ☐ Rockefeller Center
- ☐ Radio City Music Hall

- ☐ 9/11 Memorial and Museum
- ☐ Madison Square Garden
- ☐ Sightseeing Bus Tour
- ☐ Fifth Avenue
- ☐ Grand Central Station
- ☐ St. Patrick's Cathedral
- ☐ Wall Street
- ☐ Carnegie Hall

Add Your Own:

- ☐ _____
- ☐ _____
- ☐ _____
- ☐ _____
- ☐ _____
- ☐ _____
- ☐ _____

Favorites

Favorite Place I Visited:

Favorite Things I Saw:

Favorite Day of the Trip:

New Experiences

Something I Learned:

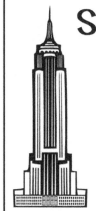

Someone I Met:

Something I Did for the First Time:

Fun Stuff

 **Souvenirs:**

Best Food I Ate:

Strangest Thing I Saw:

Moments to Remember

Part 2: Trip Journal

Made in the USA
Las Vegas, NV
13 October 2021

32269555R00072